My Life and Other

Misadventures

My Life and Other Misadventures

Alan Rick

Copyright and Ordering

First Printing: 2016
ISBN #: 978-1-326-46683-1
A L Rick

Publisher: SWit'CH
Swinton Writers in t'Critchley House
Critchley House,
Chorley Rd,
Swinton,
Manchester
M27 4AF
United Kingdom

Ordering Information:

For details, contact the publisher at the above listed address.
E-mail: switchswinton@gmail.com

SWitCH – Swinton Writers in t'Critchley House - is a community writing group encouraging members to develop writing and associated skills including, but not limited to, proof reading, editing, publishing.
http://www.switchwriters.btck.co.uk/

Preface

I suppose that when one looks back to the early years of one's life a wry chuckle is in order. Events which were not particularly amusing at the time take on a comic aspect upon mature reflection. That is my excuse for these memoirs which, if they afford the reader some entertainment, will have served their purpose.

My early years were peopled by characters of surreal eccentricity. If they had any inkling of this themselves they would have laughed too – but they remained blissfully oblivious to their own personas.

There are two main types of ignorance, the arrogant type and the innocent variety. My relatives were blessed with the latter.

Acknowledgements

Without the help of some painstaking people, this volume could not have got off the ground. In no particular order, I name my daughter Gillian who, on top of a lifetime of handling me, organised the typing and binding. The typing was done by her PA Gillian Riding. Thank you so much.

To good friend Bill Cameron and all at the SWit'CH writing group, my appreciation of their work in setting the publication process in train. A truly valuable contribution.

To my friends at the Bury writers group, many thanks for allowing me to read every chapter to them. Indulgence beyond the call of duty.

I could not possibly forget Cherryl Evans who not only read the book in draft form, but has urged me to write volume two. A special friend going back many years. To my friends in Pendle Hamlet who urged me to publish - obviously I am capable of doing as I am told.

Last but certainly not least, my very good friend Rachel Crane, who not only read the book in draft, but has tenaciously insisted I follow it with a sequel. If I know Rachel, she will not let go until I do.

Alan Rick December 2015

Contents

INTRODUCTION

Pre-war London was where I was born; to be more precise I first stared warily at my surroundings in the officers' military hospital in Woolwich, near to my parents' first (of many) fleeting residences. It is reported that I gave vent to a torrent of red faced bawling – exercising the infant lungs, the nurse said – but I am inclined to put this down to the start of a life-long distaste for all things martial. London in 1933 had not yet thought of war as a serious possibility and some of my earliest recollections were of sedate afternoon visits to Lyon's Corner House in the Strand where I was urged to sit in glum silence whilst my mother and an aunt chatted over pots of tea and cakes – this last item being the only reason I could see for coming. There was always an orchestra playing, the members of which always put me in mind of inflated black beetles in their tailcoats and starched white shirt fronts. No megadecibel jukebox trampling over all attempted conversation then; a real orchestra playing instruments and prim waitresses in black dresses and white "pinnies" and white lace caps gliding between the tables.

My first day at school was a sharply administered lesson in shock tactics. I was not told I was going there and on being deposited at the door of this awesome new world by my mother and grandmother, I promptly turned into a bundle of incandescent infant wrath. They, startled by what promised to develop into an ugly scene, just as promptly fled.

It was here that I discovered my complete incapacity to grasp arithmetic. This lasted right through to later Grammar School and beyond, and the changing of the name to Mathematics on the way did nothing to help To this day I remain only marginally more numerate than the average ten year old. The war brought evacuation for my brother and me to Derby – dismissively referred to by our primary school teachers as "The North" – and this was another culture shock I will return to in later pages.

The immediate post 1945 years in London were bleak enough. The black-out was discontinued as were the bombs, but rationing continued to a lessening degree for some time after the end of the war. But at least the many bombed out houses and public buildings afforded us boys the ideal chance for exploration and that most daring of all furtive activities – a secret smoke. By this time my brother and I had lost count of the number of homes we

had had – nothing to do with the bombing but just our parents' instinctive tendency to move house on a sheer impulse - could almost be the subject of a book all by itself. To my father, a family was not so much an integrated unit as a sort of loose confederation. In 1945 we came to roost at my grandmother's house where – perversely – we actually managed to stay for five years. Here my grandmother held uneasy sway over a discordant array of aunts, uncles, my mother and us two boys. My father was usually abroad administering Britain's rapidly fading Empire and appeared only from time to time. This period contained all the eccentric madness of Mr Vincent Crummles circus troupe, in fact had Dickens stayed with us for a while he would have been reaching for his notebook every few minutes. The sort of comic genius that produced Mrs Gamp and Mrs Nickleby was daily personified in my grandmother and my mother respectively. Against overwhelming odds and in the face of discouragement from some, I found the two lasting passions of my life, books and music.

Since then I have never felt able to recommend to the young that they listen to the advice of their elders. Much of my time was spent in the Tottenham Public Library and in the Albert Hall when I could get tickets for the concerts there. Sir Thomas Beecham, Toscanini and Bruno Walter were great names in the world of conducting and the ones who held me in thrall.

After Grammar School my country decided that it needed me. It must surely have had second thoughts when I presented myself for an interview and army medical, but still insisted that I embark on two years of very unmartial National Service. I survived this to the astonishment of both myself and a succession of very irate NCO's, who could not understand how my father – a Lieutenant Colonel with a distinguished record – could possibly have been instrumental in producing someone like me. It seemed an outrage, and on the whole, I did not feel able to dissent from this view. I was sent to Egypt and we were told we were guarding the Suez Canal from those dark forces that were always supposed to be threatening British interests in the Middle East. I remember thinking how unsafe it was in my hands but kept tactfully silent. A year or so after my return to England in December 1953 Britain finally evacuated her entire 80,000 strong force from Egypt. Perhaps they found they could not manage without me after all.

After National Service came two months in a firm of

solicitors which was a happy and untypically settled time, and then began the period which lies outside the scope of this book when something resembling achievement can here be recorded if only in brief. My talent for foreign languages prompted me to work abroad in the foreign travel business followed by marriage and a daughter and an honours degree in history (medieval and modern). The long expressed desire of my relatives that I should enter the ranks of professional people was finally satisfied I suppose when I qualified. Mathematics had not held me back after all. Now many years and 14 homes later would I like to experience it all again? Yes, but I would require advance notice of certain periods so I could be anaesthetised first.

My father, Lt Col Leonard Rick – Administering the Empire

1 – THE FIRST DAY AT SCHOOL -A RUDE AWAKENING

Well this was a culture shock without a doubt. Here I was being escorted by my mother and grandmother through the street and to the gates of the courtyard of a building the size of which my child's mind had never imagined before.

At the gates I was handed over to a gaunt lady who was

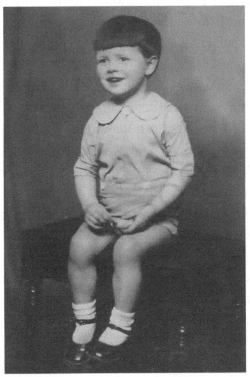

pacing up and down like a camp guard. I looked behind me. Why were my relatives already disappearing round the corner of the street as if anxious to escape from the scene of a crime? I looked up at the lady whose hand mine was seemingly glued to and uttered a protest.

"Now, now," she murmured her face portraying that lethal combination of kindness and steel, the trademark of primary school teachers of the period, "We don't make a fuss because we're a big boy aren't we?" I was later to learn that angelic behaviour qualified you for the title of "big boy" – bad conduct condemned you to "little boy" status as in "silly little boy", "awkward little boy" and so on. I imagined there existed somewhere a glossary of educational terms containing a complete list of prefixes to the word boy that could be varied according to the situation.

We soon came to the main entrance over which was engraved in the stonework 'Coleraine Infant School'. This then, quite unknown to me until that moment, was to be my first day at school. Quickly I was led to a classroom containing about 30 impossibly quiet children, and was handed over to Miss Hedge who held sway imperiously over her charges. The silence was easily explained by her demeanour which resembled a time bomb likely to explode at the slightest provocation. One small boy who had already lit the fuse was in the corner facing the wall with hands on head. The rest, like so many jars, were having knowledge about plants and trees poured into them. Miss Hedge, a lady of indestructible virtue, built like a fortress against the hand of man, made the mistake of sitting me next to a blue-ribboned, pink-dressed girl called Jennifer. This was fatal and hostility soon welled up inside me like a rising tidal wave. Soon she turned to me with an expression of massive smugness, her nose elevated to a position roughly midway between the top of my head and the ceiling.

"I get special privileges. I'm the milk monitor." That did it. What were the turbulent thoughts and feelings inside my head, all jostling with each other and dying to escape and hurl themselves at her? The outcome was swift and decisive. I decided she was a snob. Well it stood to reason: a girl with a name like Jennifer must be: normal girls had names like – well Doris or Gwen. Spurred on by my brilliant analysis of the social system, I felt that action was called for and promptly dealt her a blow to the shoulder that reduced her to tears on the spot.

"Now that was not very friendly was it little man – we don't hit each other, it does not do" intoned the fortress with an expression roughly midway between smiling encouragement and veiled menace.

I was placed at a desk alone at a safe distance from the others like a quarantined patient. During the course of the day groups of other teachers came to peer at me. It seemed that I was interesting. They would murmur amongst themselves, there would be grave nodding of heads, they would bend over me like tall trees, and their faces coming down towards me from what seemed a tremendous height as I looked skywards at them. I had no idea what was happening as one particularly tall tree took out his spectacles, arranged them precariously on the end of his nose and bent down to examine me. I felt like a rare, exotic species in a laboratory as the nodding and murmuring went on. And always those relentless smiles like a label pinned onto the face for the child's benefit to be removed when no longer required. Apparently this was called

'Cognitive Child Centred Psychology', a dark art which was just beginning to make its way into educational thinking at that time. It seemed that I was a project which made me important, though not in any way I could understand.

As for Jennifer, I noted with deep satisfaction that she was still intermittently sobbing though on the way to being mollified with a bar of chocolate.

I now had time to reflect on the various titles bestowed upon me during the course of the day. "Big boy" – "little boy" – and then "little man" well all rather confusing of course, but still I mused as I noticed Jennifer rubbing her shoulder – 'a little man has to do what a little man has to do.'

2 – THE BIRTHDAY PARTY

I suppose the children's birthday party is one of the earliest events that stay in the mind forever. These spectacles, organised as much for the parents themselves as for the children, made possible the display of the offspring in all their gaudy finery. It required the sort of lengthy and thorough preparation of the child that borders on the sadistic. The event I was dragooned into was the birthday of Janet, a little girl across the street. It seemed a slight enough cause to me considering the ordeal I was put through beforehand. This was to be scrubbed from head to foot, whiter than some peoples' doorsteps, to have my hair vandalised to reduce it to an acceptable length, to be decked out in clothes that I thought were only worn by dolls and to be on the receiving end of a moral lecture concerning manners, conduct and unattainable objectives. A small spirited boy was not meant for any of this I thought, as I glumly submitted to the strange preoccupations of the adult world. But perhaps the party itself would provide opportunities to sabotage it – we would see.

These parties followed a certain ritual – one shook the hand of Janet, with an air of feigned cordiality, and murmured a few words of courtesy, memorised from my mother's list drilled into me earlier that day.

The children, garbed as if at some exotic festival, were seated round a circular table eying the goodies, their eyes growing larger by the minute. Any attempt to touch any until the starting signal was firmly restrained by the parents, ranged like a circle of prison guards.

My mother's preparation for a party included the lecture concerning manners, conduct and unattainable objectives

---

The parents had their own agenda in all of this, which was to secure two hours of peace and quiet while the children were engaged in the absorbing task of filling their faces. Nowadays this would be achieved by the irritating means of the Computer game. His or her room will be turned into a mass of wires and plugs and screens, the child will be wired up and plugged into about 40 controls worldwide and can spend the next two hours shouting at about three million children round the globe. Not in my day. At a party you just filled each child with about 3 times its weight in jelly, gave it a lump of play dough (then called Plasticine) and retired to put your feet up. Simple.

There was that wonderful moment during this party when Janet's mother, oozing maternal bliss from every pore, came round to each of us in turn with a large plate of cakes. At last, a reason for being here; grown-ups were not all wrath and finger wagging then and I had my fair share of greed. There were benefits in allowing the backs of your ears to be inspected and even your hair combed. At last the lady of the house approached me – this promised to be my lime-lit moment.

"And which cake would you like little Alan?" she gushed with a smile.

"The biggest." I answered benignly.

My mother's face assumed the pallor of deep winter frost, the prison guards shifted uneasily and the laughter from the other children sounded like a gurgling drain.

Later that day at home the consequences were dire but not lasting. Would I try to sabotage adult morality again? No – the price was too high and, in any case I would have to join them one day.

3 – EVACUATION - NORTH AND SOUTH
DIVIDED BY A COMMON LANGUAGE

It was during the last year of the war in 1944 that it finally seemed to dawn on the government that hostility had commenced and hastily had us London children packed off to the provinces to escape the V2 rockets – Hitler's last gasp attempt to grab victory. My brother and I had no idea what evacuation entailed beyond our teacher's vague and disdainful explanation that we would be banished to 'The North'. This, we gathered, was some sort of limbo land you were sent to if you were seen as no longer fit for civilised society. But at least it would be better than the bombs. We were prepared for the first stage of the journey to the railway station for transportation to we had no idea where by the teacher, Mr Redman, who was not allowed to tell us the destination. This acquired an even more sinister aspect in our minds when we learnt that he would not be staying there but would be returning to London once he had delivered us to the families who had agreed to take in evacuees.

Why were our parents to remain in London? We were convinced that we must have committed some grave misbehaviour to be sent parentless to what may as well have been a foreign country. Any place, in our minds, north of Middlesex was threatening territory.

Suitably dressed for travel in coats, trousers and shirts mainly handed down from older siblings and with boxed gas masks secured to our sides, we were marched to the railway station for our voyage into the unknown, a bedraggled picture of bewilderment and distrust. The government manufacturer of gas masks had ordered special, smaller versions to be made for primary school children. Mine had a Mickey Mouse on the outside, apparently intended to mark the child size gas mask. The cautionary gas mask drill exercise was supervised by the Headmaster who would strike fear into us by describing, with staring eyed relish, how mustard gas would get into our lungs. This meant that we would have just two and a half minutes at most to fit the contraption over our face to save our lives. Armed with a whistle like a race official at a dog track he would then time us. In the event the Germans didn't use mustard gas this time - having decided that bombing from the air would cause us more discomfort. I owe the fact that I am still here to this as my lamentable efforts to get the mask on in the allotted time would have consigned me to an early oblivion.

Eventually the train, the steam puffer type, reached Derby. It was a revelation to us to discover that "The North" was not just a vast wasteland after all, but had towns in it including the one we were decanted at i.e. Derby. Our first meeting point was the Town Hall, where we again lined up and numbers placed on our chests by way of identification so that the families who had ordered us could see which children they were getting. Soon the families themselves were called in and began to look along the line of evacuees to claim their prize and cart him or her home. Their faces registered the whole gamut of responses from delighted through to disappointment to appalled, according to whether or not they liked the look of what they were getting. Altogether it seemed like a cross between a cattle market and an auction sale.

Our new home for the rest of the war was a house on the outskirts of Derby and was inhabited by a couple whose own daughter was married and had gone to live elsewhere. We were lucky in that they were kind and did not have young children at home to compare us unfavourably with. There were others who were not so lucky. The husband was a keen fisherman, the river Derwent flowed nearby and there were silver cups behind a glass case in the living room – which they called 'the best room'. The word 'lounge' had not yet come into general use except in the more exalted classes. I was to accompany the husband and his friends on Sunday mornings to fish in the Derwent. Many a tale was recounted about the 'one that got away' which always seemed to be bigger than any of those that were caught.

Fitting into a new home with temporary parents was a surprisingly smooth transition, but starting a new school was not. First there was the accent. Many and loud were the heated assertions in the playground the we 'sootheners' had the wrong one. Why did they say 'coop of tea' instead of 'cap of tea' was only one of the issues hotly disputed? Neither side would give way on any of this item of fierce regional pride and the matter was always concluded – though never decided – by a fight with anything up to a dozen joining in. This was when I discovered that England is a country divided by a common language.

Another major problem was the Derby children's complete misunderstanding of what the word 'evacuee' meant. They were convinced that we had been sent out of London on account of some minor criminal activity on our part. What did you do? This was the question often shot at us, and great was the disappointment when we were not able to produce examples of lurid delinquency to explain our appearance in 'The North'. The experience was especially galling to the cockney children of the dockland area of the East End, whose only fault was to live near the Port of London docks and, as in many cases, to have been bombed out of their homes. Their contribution to the linguistic divide was not just their fists, which they deployed in a manner marvellous to behold, but an outpouring of language so colourful that some were sent home with a note to say that they would be allowed back into school only on condition of acceptable behaviour.

If Derby was expecting genteel decorum from East End children who had had a hard life, who had been bombed out and now were being teased in the playground, then Derby would be disappointed.

One ginger haired boy, one of Dickens legions of the 'great unsoaped', stood up in class and exclaimed "F*** this for a lark", treated all present with the reverse V for victory gesture and walked out. He was later retrieved by the police having set out with a little bundle of belongings on the road leading out of Derby, which he imagined led all the way to London.

All in all there were lessons to be learnt from evacuation. The English language is a glorious dialectical muddle which is why we have a great literary heritage. We were able to take criticism on board and the real eye opener was that there actually was sentient life further north than Middlesex. Even trains travelled further up than that.

We returned home in the Spring of 1945 when the war ended, to the same primary school we had left a year earlier and to the same teachers who told us how lucky we were not to have been under Nazi occupation. Even the teasing about our accents was better than bombs. I have remembered their words ever since. In the cinema in Tottenham High Road film shots, just released by the government of the newly liberated death camps of Belsen and Auschwitz left us with a profound sense of both the sufferings of the victims and of our good fortune in being free.

4 – OUR GRANDMOTHER

Bomb damaged London was the ideal environment for Nan to display her own blend of abrasive resilience: we often got the impression that the Second World War was some sort of personal struggle between herself and Hitler.

She was a typical product of her time. She looked like a puppet doll from the window of a shop that deals in Victorian bric-a-brac. She still wore the style of clothes you can see in old film footage about the time of the Boer War. Black dress down to the ankles, lace collar, black as if permanently in mourning, and a straw hat of the same colour with a flower in the side of it for walking out. This was my grandmother.

She was of slightly below average height, sparse of frame, and always walked with a look of intense purpose – looking straight ahead as if in pursuit of some quarry. She was a good listener but had, to us two boys, a disconcerting way of inclining her head to one side, bird like, while she listened as if she did not quite believe what she was being told. She was, as it seemed to us, excessively upright, given her age and always urged us boys to do likewise with the words "Never could abide a boy who can't stand upright!" The list of things that Nan could "never abide in a boy" was impressive and included talking with your mouth full, laughing at your own jokes, and raising one's voice above a certain level. In point of fact, during this period of food rationing it was seldom that the mouth managed to get full in any case.

She was described by our uncle George as a 'sturdy trooper', which meant that she had a mind conditioned by the rationing and shortages of that time. Many years after the end of food rationing and the return of plenty, she would still explain with a startled look,

"Go steady with that pot of jam – it's all there is to last the weekend."

History had passed her by – she was both the mother and the grandmother of all eccentrics. She would accept no criticism of her actions, however bizarre.

One day she announced that she had made us a rice pudding to celebrate the fact that rice had become available again. The huge bowl was borne in state from the kitchen like the Holy Grail but one glance into it showed that it was just a bowl of hot milk.

"But" we cried in despair, "You've, forgotten to put the rice in!"

"Get it down you and don't complain." She shot back with a disdainful shrug. The war had shown her that complaining was of no use.

During the blitz on London we slept under the stairs, in the Anderson shelter and, at her insistence, under the dining room table.

"That table will stop anything." She would assert. "It's solid English Oak."

We had this heroic picture in our minds of the house reduced to rubble, but of our dining room table still standing as a proud monument to defiance.

The owner of the grocer's shop was completely terrorised by Nan, for some extra portions over and above the weekly food ration.

"I've got two hungry boys at home." Nan would shout.

"Everybody has hungry boys at home." He would reply with a despairing look at the ceiling.

"Miserable old devil." She muttered.

In those days we had open coal fires in the house. This gave Nan her chance to enjoy her Guinness, mulled or heated.

"Taken only for my health you know."

This involved standing a glass of Nan's sacred nectar on the table, then all of us standing well clear as she plunged the red hot end of a poker into it so that it fizzed and swelled like a steam engine. We would cower against the wall at this macabre performance which could have been the famous witches' scene from Macbeth.

This was also the period when American soldiers toting

the coveted chewing gum, were stationed in our part of London. They also introduced nylon stockings – the wonder of the age – and, inevitably, some of our housewives strayed into their arms. The struggle between upright morality and the exotic lure of shear nylon was sometimes an unequal one. One such lady lived in our street, cold shouldered by the rest of the women, and representing something else that Nan 'could not abide'. My brother and I summoned the courage to ask Nan why this lady was always being talked about in hushed tones across the garden fences, and how she managed to acquire such a splendid array of material goods at a time of acute national shortage. It was generally agreed among the more lethal of the local housewives that there were dresses of a dubious cost and of even more dubious origin – jewellery of various kinds and, it was darkly hinted, a fur coat. The garden fences resonated with this louche intelligence like some malevolent telegraph system. Nan searched for a suitable answer – she belonged to the seen-but-not-heard school of child rearing. We pressed her and, at last, looking straight at some point two feet above our heads, she gave it.

"She's doing her bit for the war effort!"

It was to be many years before the meaning if this opaque statement was to become clear to us.

5 – REX – THE PHILOSOPHER KING

I suppose most children must see their relatives as inhabitants of a benign world of eccentricity. Mine, headed by my grandmother, were no exception. But my aunty Gladys, a lady of surreal thinking, managed to dispense with rational thought altogether and plunge into a mental world which none of us was ever able to penetrate.

She was that specialist home-grown product of English soil – the doting animal lover. Her own pride and joy was Rex – a shambling pile of canine fur with no particular looks to speak of and no discernible purpose in life other than to amble through each day as it came. But to aunt Gladys, though to no-one else, there was far more to Rex than this. We would often be treated to examples of his vast intellect.

"Be careful what you talk about," we were cautioned "He understands every word you say."

We looked at Rex for evidence of this but this always escaped us since all Rex ever did was to fix the opposite wall with a baleful stare.

"He's thoughtful," aunt Gladys would add as we expressed doubt concerning his famed powers of reasoning. "He's considering things."

Much as we tried to picture Rex as the Philosopher King or as some sort of canine Confucius, the attempt was always dashed by the fact that all he ever did was to stare morosely at the opposite wall. He could hardly have derived inspiration from the wall which was covered with dull, brown wallpaper with no pattern on it.

"He's having an idea." Our aunt would insist. Apparently

whenever Rex stared, this meant that he was "having an idea". Following this bizarre logic, his head must have been as full as an overpopulated beehive, as staring was all he ever did.

The truth was that Rex had only two ideas – to eat, to accompany the staring, when food was placed in front of him and to sleep when it was not!

All criticism of Rex was spurned by his deluded owner on the grounds that he was "Subject to deep emotional feelings."

"He's sensitive you know, he gets upset if people say unkind things about him."

Again we would look at Rex for signs of emotional turbulence, for outbursts against injustices spoken against him but he just stared at the wall. Rex was as emotional as a wax figure – compared to Rex the goldfish was beside itself. The fish would gently waft its tail in an elegant and quite expressive gesture. Rex stared. There was no poetry in Rex.

In time Rex became slower in his movements, if that were possible, until even staring at the wall seemed to demand more effort than he was able to summon. He ended his days before a roaring open fire. It was then that our aunt felt able to disclose to us what, it seemed, had often passed between them in our absence.

"He sometimes had some sorry words to say about you two boys when you used to scoff at his lively mind."

So Rex could talk as well!

It's often said, quite rightly, that our pet animals should be well looked after, but perhaps there are cases where the owner should be 'taken into care' as well.

6 – THE RETREAT

Any visit to my Aunt Mabel's house offered one pleasure only. This was the room she called "The Retreat". Solitary and sad, like a long abandoned relative, it lay sulking in the topmost corner of the house at the end of a landing to which it seemed to have been flung by my aunt during one of her fits of volcanic temper. Do not misunderstand me, Aunt Mabel was a fervent advocate of world peace but she made an exception in the case of her own household, which would be a constant war zone.

To me only, would this room yield its secrets. In this room, as if into an indoor council tip, had been stacked everything that was unwanted by Aunt Mabel over a period of some thirty years. From one wall a photograph, minus the dignity of a frame, of her still living but surplus to requirements husband, stared glumly at the door, a prisoner now in pictorial effigy. A cricket bat of my uncle's, like him now wizened by age and constant misuse, seemed to find it an effort to remain standing against the opposite wall, its spirit also broken.

The room had one window facing the garden. From this it would have obtained the only light to raise its crushed spirits had my aunt not had wooden shutters fitted. These enclosing bars informed the inmates, that the world outside had no further interest in them, that they should rest and moulder, and be grateful that a small boy, untouched by memories should delight in their fading charms.

Why were this room and its deteriorating contents special to me? Had they not once had a vigorous life of their own? Had the cricket bat not fronted my uncle's glittering skill at the wicket? Where were the applause and the acclaim now? This decaying bric-a-brac had once been paraded by my two relatives as vibrant symbols of the life they had shared – the cricket bat – instrument of my uncle's bravado at the crease; the half-finished special drawings – witness to my aunt's long vanished desire to shine in the galleries of London's West End.

It was beyond the understanding of a small boy as he gazed about him in this cluttered room, that a decayed marital bond should relegate its symbols to oblivion. I wanted to take them all out of that room, mount them on a huge stand and let them proudly proclaim, "We, at least are still alive."

7 – LITTLE FREDA

Little Freda Rosenthal came into our North London primary school shortly before the curtain came down on the Second World War. She was from Austria and, being already a talented musician, had a deep love for her homeland, the land of Mozart and Schubert. Sadly Austria no longer loved her. She was Jewish and the Nazis had decided that the Jews were beyond the pale.

She sat in class quietly introspective, enveloped in a wistful melancholy but never complaining about anything. I remember thinking, as we children moaned about this and that being "not fair" how stoical this little girl was to never give way to the feelings she must have had. I did not realise then that she had matters on her mind that dwarfed our petty complaints.

Her parents were still in Vienna. They had succeeded in spiriting Freda out of the country with the help of sympathetic officers but had not been allowed to escape themselves.

They undertook to write to Freda every week via the neutral Swiss Post Office but, if the letters should suddenly stop, then she must forget her mother and father and enjoy her chance of a life of freedom and respect in England.

The letters continued for some time and then stopped. Why? We can all guess what had been the certain fate of her parents. She never heard from them again.

Soon afterwards I passed the assembly hall at school on my way to the classroom and heard the sounds of the slow movement of the Beethoven Moonlight Sonata. I peered into the hall and saw Freda at the grand piano filling the air with the velvet tones of this soothing music. Out of the ugly profanity of evil she had conjured up the benign.

It was too much for me and I melted silently into tears. Then I felt the hand of Mr Ayling, the Headmaster, upon my shoulder. "Steady on old chap." He gently intoned. This was still the time when a boy was not expected to succumb to emotions but should 'be a man'.

Freda had shamed me with her stead-fastness in the face of the awful. She had far more reason for tears than I could possibly lay claim to yet, we never saw any. We never saw any.

8 – THE RIVER LEA

The River Lea meanders through the North London Tottenham marshes. It has an air as if remembering that day back in the ninth century when the Saxon King Alfred met Guthrum, the chief of the invading Vikings, who were bent on marching west through Alfred's territory – the Kingdom of Wessex. On the banks of this river the treaty was signed between them which confirmed the land to the west as Alfred's and that to the East as belonging to Guthrum and his fierce warriors. To the Danelaw in Yorkshire was added another permanent settlement of Viking stock in the South East. A huge amount of water has flown between these banks since those turbulent times and what a dramatic story would the river have been able to tell had she the power of speech.

As a small boy I loved the river and its routine activities before mechanisation abolished most of them. The barges, still towed by Shire horses clip clopping along the tow path, the sluice gates being opened and shut to let them through and the solitary men seated at respectful intervals along the bank hoping the fish would reward their superhuman patience with a bite as they morosely cast and recast their rods. The water was much less poisoned by industrial waste then than now so there were fish to be had. I often thought that staring at the water for so many hours at a time surely deserved some reward. Through the eyes of a small boy all these sights were never to be missed and I was on the banks most days on my way home from school to watch and wonder. These natural human sights satisfied me in a way that computer games, had they existed, could not have done. We had none of the wonders of technology now available to today's children yet we were never bored. The radio, then called the wireless, the local cinema – there were five in Tottenham High Road alone – and Tottenham Hotspur Football Club. Tottenham Hotspur Football Club on a Saturday afternoon was enough sustenance for us.

One of the sights that caught my attention one day was a man fishing by the bank. I stopped to hear his companion waxing eloquently about the day's catch or rather the lack of it. Actually the language was hardly eloquent as it introduced my innocent ears to the F word for the first time in my life. There was never swearing in my family or among my relatives at all so it came as something of a shock when I later discovered the gravity of it.

I arrived just as one man was asking the other if he had any luck that day.

"Nah been here all day and haven't caught a f**king thing." He replied.

There didn't seem to be any reason to stay any longer. And continued on my way home. It was a Sunday afternoon and the scene was being set where we lived during the war years at the house of my grandmother for the Sunday tea. There were always several relatives present for the occasion mainly so that they could all pool their food rations to make up one, quite impressive food pile considering that these were straitened times. The rationing of food was not exactly generous. Seated around the table were my grandmother, like some ominous matriarch that the Victorian era had forgotten to

28

take with it when it ended, my mother, my father home on extended leave from India, two aunts and two uncles. I found myself sitting next to Aunt Mabel. Aunt Mabel was an incurable snob with pretentions to gentility. She thought that the sole purpose of education was to teach a child to speak "naaaaacily". It mattered not if it didn't have an idea in its head – appearance was all.

During the course of the long awaited, though sparse, meal she turned to me and enquired with that seraphic smile for which she was well known.

"Have you had a nice day Alan?"

"Yes I went along the Lea and met two men fishing."

"Oh that was nice and had they caught a lot of fish?"

"No, they hadn't, in fact one said the other, let me see, yes he said, I've been here all day and not caught a f**king thing."

There followed an ice bound silence, the atmosphere in the room assumed the air of a deep winter frost, there was pursing of lips from Aunt Mabel, awkward shuffling of feet under the table, one of them aimed accurately at my shin. What had I said? It shows how innocent we were in those days that I didn't even know it was a swear word! Seeing the general discomfort into which the room was now plunged, I burst into tears and fled upstairs into the safety of my own room.

Sometime later I heard footsteps on the stairs. This proved to be my father and an uncle. I spluttered my apologies even though I had no idea what I had done.

"It's nothing to worry about," my father assured me, "but that word you came out with – we don't use it in company."

By way of comfort in my obvious distress, he gave me half a crown which went some way to alleviating my feelings. As they went downstairs again I could hear my father say to my uncle;

"It was worth it, wasn't it, just to see Mabel's face."

9 - WARTIME RATIONING AND CHILDREN'S FUN

Life at Grandma's house was not made easier during the War years by the fact that food was rationed and allocated to each individual member of the public on a very strict but well organised basis. It was explained to my brother and me that the cause of all this outrage, as we saw it, was the irritating habit the German U boats had of sinking our merchant shipping at sea and allowing only a limited amount of food to be imported. This seemed a poor excuse to us boys; all we knew was that we were hungry! Each member of the public was issued with a ration book. The inside page was divided into fifty two numbered squares representing the weeks of the year. This had to be produced to the shopkeeper, there were very few supermarkets then, who would cut out one square and provide us with the very small ration of each type of food. The missing square meant you could not go back for more until the following week. The system was very well organised by the Ministry of Food under Lord Woolton, and ensured that although nobody got very much, everyone got just enough to live on. The penalties were severe for any shopkeeper caught giving a customer more than their ration because if this became widespread, then some people would be deprived of their entitlement. Any shopkeeper who transgressed risked the wrath of the authorities.

One such succumbed to temptation when two officials posing as customers asked for more food, intimating that they had money in their pockets to give him. The grocer agreed and the moment the money passed across the counter, they pulled out their identification cards from their pockets and declared, "Board of Trade, you are under arrest." It earned him a prison sentence.

Our Grandma was a sturdy rebel against the rationing system, seeing it as a sort of demonic conspiracy by the government to keep the population under control.

"They like to keep you under," she would intone darkly. Her opposition took the form of terrorising the local shopkeeper vainly to give more than the ration book allowed.

"I've got two hungry boys at home," she would rant.

"Everyone has two hungry boys at home," came the anguished reply.

It was a fruitless verbal duel as this grocer was only too mindful of the penalties for cheating to be fool enough to cooperate.

My brother Brian and I
there are always two hungry boys at home.

It is strange how measures brought in as "temporary" for a specific emergency tend to linger long after the crisis has ended. Income tax is an example: initiated to pay for the Napoleonic Wars, it has somehow managed to stay with us down to the present day! So it was with rationing. The war ended in 1945 but the rationing managed to continue to 1954 when sweets and chocolates were freed. The reason behind the delay in freeing the last two items was that they were not a necessity – a claim stoutly denied by my brother and me. A common sight in the playground was an entrepreneurial pupil sidling up to us with a conspiratorial air and a quick sideways glance, wishing to know if we wanted to buy some sweet coupons he had probably acquired from a relative who never ate sweets.

Of course rationed goods, including clothes, could always be obtained at an exorbitant price on the black market, but we were never allowed to deal with it. My father was of the opinion that those who ran it and profiteered by it should be shot.

One huge difference between that era and today is how we children entertained ourselves. In those days before the wonders of Information Technology and computer games, we were thrown back on our own resources for our amusement. In the home everything centred on the radio – they called the 'wireless', and externally there was the weekly visit to the cinema – then called the 'pictures'. Television had been invented – the world's first transmission went out from Alexandra Palace in London in 1936 but in our time some 10 years later no one had yet acquired a set. We did know one couple nearby who actually had a set and if a big event was being shown – such as the wedding of Princess Elizabeth and the Duke of Edinburgh in 1947, the whole street would gather in their living room to watch.

This was the true heyday of the cinema before television began to close cinemas up and down the country. Tottenham High Road had eight cinemas at one time! It was such an institution that you had to queue up taking your place in one of three different priced queues to get in. The Palace cinema even had a splendid uniformed doorman to manage the queues smiling ingratiatingly as he escorted the patrons in and sternly ordering the ones in the cheap queue to "stand back you lot." The class system was alive and well! The fare on offer was generous. There were two films, the 'big film' and a secondary one. During the interval an organist played some of the 'much loved ones' and attractive usherettes came down the aisle with a tray of ice-cream. Banter, even during the film, was acceptable. I remember one well-loved wag who always sat in the front row who would upbraid a father laying down the law to a rebellious daughter with, "She's over 21."

No primary school playground was complete without several games of 'five stones' known to us as 'gobs' in progress. You had five small, square shaped coloured stones which were tossed into the air in a variety of permutations progressively more difficult. This was also the era when cigarette manufacturers put a coloured picture card into the back of the cigarette packet to encourage sales. It's hard to imagine this being encouraged today but at that time the films portrayed the stars as smoking a cigarette – it was what we would describe as 'cool'. We youngsters could collect a whole set of English monarchs or footballers or whatever set was on offer. Many a parent or relative was cajoled into buying another packet so that we could complete a set. It always seemed to the unwitting, we hoped, parent that we were just one card short to complete the set. But the cards had another purpose for us boys. They could, in competition with another boy, be flicked up against the wall of the playground and whichever card bounced back further away from the wall was confiscated by the winner.

Marbles – or 'alleys' as we called them, were rolled along the gutter of the pavement in the street and were greatly prized as they came in many beautiful colours. Sadly this, together with hopscotch on the pavement and the cricket match in the middle of the street using the lamppost as a wicket, have long since vanished, the enormous increase in cars since then have made it impossible, even in a side road.

Which generation was the happier? I don't think there is a simple answer to this and, in any case, it must be subjective. If you see material possessions as the source of happiness then you will no doubt conclude that today's young are happier. Against this must be mentioned that we did not miss it as much of it had not been invented in our time. The simple amusements requiring no sophisticated technology that we enjoyed will seem quaint now but gave us the sort of self-fulfilling pleasure that has been lost. The consumer society promises more and more possessions but never delivers satisfaction, only the desire for more of them.

10 - MY RELATIVES

My aunt Gwen was steady, unremarkable and in all respects what is considered to be a normal member of society. In this she managed to stand out from the rest of my relations who displayed all the colourful traits of surrealism you would expect to see on display in a residential home for the slightly unhinged.

There was my aunt Gladys who, together with her dog Rex, has the distinction of a chapter of her own in this work. She would insist that she had mislaid things in Australia if only one of us would go there and retrieve them. She had never been to Australia and, needless to say, there was no stampede from us to volunteer to undertake the quest. She even went to the extent of writing to the Governor of Australia to elicit his help. There was no reply.

My uncle Bill was a fervent admirer of the arts by proxy. He had never read a book in his life nor heard any music other than the latest popular song but would impress upon my brother and I the absolute need to take note of Shakespeare and of Beethoven because they were 'marvellous'. He always referred to the paintings of the great masters as 'photos' even though photography had not yet been invented in their time. It was in vain that we boys tried to point out an error of fact on his part; his response was to eye us in a pitying manner and to inform us with an air of massive condescension, that we would "understand better when we grew up."

No more be said about Grandma she is well

documented within these pages and was perhaps the fountain of all eccentricity in the family.

A special accolade must go to aunt Mabel. She was an incurable snob and a firm believer in class distinction. Her views on education reflected this; holding that if it is paid for privately that it must be better. Together with this went the notion that if a child could 'speak nicely' then that was all that was required from an education. There was much pursing of the lips from her when the Labour Party won the landslide victory in the 1945 election, declaring that "the country won't stand for it."

I suppose that my uncle Bill takes the prize for the most irrational act on record. He used to go to Petticoat Lane market on Sunday mornings. On his return from one of these trips he produced an eight feet tall Red Indian totem pole complete with full decoration. My grandmother intervened when he proposed to erect it in the front garden on the not unreasonable grounds that 'it was not in keeping with a leafy North London suburb'. It made good firewood when chopped up later.

11 - First Visit to White Hart Lane

The name White Hart Lane is engraved on the mind of every one of my relatives going back several generations. It is, of course, the home ground of Tottenham Hotspur football club and the spiritual home of my family going back to my grandfather who was born two years before its foundation in 1882. Since then uncles and great uncles of mine have roared their approval of the white shirted heroes every Saturday afternoon or sometimes directing their spleen at the Arsenal whose ground at Highbury was only four miles away, and a fierce rivalry between the two clubs has flared undiminished for a century.

The time finally arrived in 1943 when, under the watchful eye of my uncle Leslie, I was to be inducted into the sacred rite of attending my first ever match. It was against Millwall and, although I do not remember who won, I can still feel the thrill of standing in the crowd of some 50,000 people and listening to the words of encouragement and of criticism expressed in alarmingly graphic terms, of the throng around me. In those days you stood in the terraces – both sets of supporters mixed together. The stand had seats and booking one in advance was seen as posh at a price of four shillings and sixpence (22p in present day money). This would only happen if the match was a special one. I recall my uncle Bill deciding to book seats for us in a cup tie against Stoke City as the legendary Stan Matthews was going to play.

In those days before technology took over information

about team changes was quite primitive. Metal plates spelling a player's name would be placed along the touchline on both sides so that all could see them. During half time the crowd was entertained by the St. John's Ambulance band marching up and down the pitch playing popular tunes with the bandsman in front tossing a decorative mace as he went. We all looked forward to the day when he would drop it but we under-estimated his skill as he never did.

This was the time when clubs were allowed to field 'guest players' as they were called even though the player was not on the clubs books. A player who was in the army – as all the fit ones were – and whose army unit was near to a club could play for that club because he could easily be called up in an emergency. It was a source of great amusement to us to see that, at one stage, the Arsenal fielded nine 'guest players' out of eleven! Highbury – Arsenal's ground at that time - was damaged by a bomb during the early part of the war and they were obliged to play all their home matches at White Hart Lane. The good natured mockery from the Spurs supporters was loud but, in those days, relatively affectionate. How times have changed.

"Oh dear, ain't you got no 'ome to go to." "Never mind, we'll put you up free of charge."

Strange situations could occur with no notice given. One Saturday morning the Spurs team found itself a player short due to the call up. A call went out on the loud speaker system asking if there was anyone in the crowd with experience of playing and, if so, would he please report to the dressing room. One such hopeful, sensing the lure of fame, did report and was duly kitted out in the Spurs' colours and kicked off with the rest of the team. It soon became hilariously clear that he had never kicked a ball in his life: every time the ball was passed to him he just fell over. The crowd loved it and gave him a roaring cheer whenever he got the ball. I doubt that such comic antics would engender the same affectionate response in today's money oriented game when everything has become deadly serious.

Another much loved character at the Lane was 'Old Down the Middle'. He would bawl at Spurs players with suggestions as to how they should proceed when they got the ball. The less competent player would have an epithet hurled at him which, to my unknowing mind, I took to be casting doubt on his parentage! It was puzzling to me and certainly the players, to hear that, whatever the situation that he had only one solution to offer. This was to boot the ball 'down the middle'. Of course neither the player nor the supporters took any notice of this and he simply became part of the entertainment. Had he stopped attending matches he would have been sorely missed by all.

This then was White Hart Lane. Not just a football ground but almost a sacred shrine for my family who came to offer worship to the white shirted gods who delighted us and had done so since the foundation of the club in 1882.

12 - JOURNEY INTO THE UNKNOWN

This is heaven for a small boy. A room set out as a playroom with colour picture bricks, toys, a chute to slide down and the walls covered with the animals from the cartoons we children loved so much. How did we get to be here? We won't bother to ask as it's far too much fun to question. But why is the number of children in this room getting less and less? Is it something to do with the nice, friendly lady in a uniform who comes in from time to time to take one child away? She seems to be friendly and yet I'm puzzled. There is surely something wrong in all this, enjoyable though it is. Why don't the missing children ever come back? I don't feel like playing anymore.

Here comes the lady in uniform again. She beckons to us two – the last two left. "Come with me dears, your turn now."

This means nothing to me and my tearful pleas are not answered except for an indulgent smile. Panic grips me as, with soothing words of comfort, I am led down a long, semi dark corridor. The walls on either side are not prettily decorated like the ones in the playroom, but are plain and seem to have been whitewashed in some way. At the end of the corridor is a closed door with word on it I don't understand. The lady still holds my hand gently though firmly. Her smile is also gentle and seemingly kind, but at the same time, declining to offer any relief to my frightened pleas.

At last she opens the door. Suddenly the dim light behind us is replaced by a brilliant shining light of the room before us.

I cover my eyes to shield them from being dazzled. The lady makes no such attempt. Is she used to it?

In the middle of the room I can see a sort of table covered with a cloth and, around it, as if they were about to examine something, are several uniformed men and women with their faces half covered with a sort of white cloth leaving only their eyes visible. Gently, with more of the soothing, words I have come to be suspicious of, I am persuaded to lie down face up on the table.

Suddenly, and without warning, a mask is placed over my face; I cannot breath and a few seconds later – oblivion.

Now, some hours later, I am awake and in bed with a sore throat. Surprised I see all the children who disappeared from the playroom earlier that day in a line of beds stretching the length of what is obviously a hospital ward. They all have sore throats too. Soon our parents come to collect us. They have instructions not to allow solid food for the next week or two. Why could we only swallow bread and milk? The government in its infinite wisdom had decreed that all children in that part of London's primary schools must have their tonsils and adenoids removed!

13 - THE BLITZ ON LONDON

They hit the city in 1940 several months after the outbreak of the war in 1939. The initial period has been described as the "phoney war" as nothing seems to have happened. This had even decided the authorities to bring the evacuees back to London as the anticipated danger seemed not to be happening. The rude awakening, however, was lurking just round the corner. Following a bombing raid on Berlin by the R.A.F., Hitler ordered a massive bombing of London by way of retaliation and also to scare the people of the city into persuading our government to sue for peace.

From the first night on the city was ablaze and the fire service was sorely stretched to keep up with it. This was specially the case with the East End which was a prime target because it was where the Port of London Docks was situated: - a key supply area from abroad. It was a distressing sight the morning after a raid to see families searching among the rubble of a flattened house or whole street, trying to find their possessions. I remember a little baby being carried out of the remains of a house by the fire service as its grief stricken parents looked on – the baby was not to see its first birthday. These things stay in the mind forever.

This was the time when the population became used to tight regulation on its movements. We had already become used to having to queue for everything. We now had to listen for the air raid sirens giving warning of an enemy raid. These sirens had two sounds; a wailing sound to alert us and a continuous sound on one note when the danger was over.

Houses were instructed to be 'blackened out'. This involved covering the windows with cloths after dark so that the enemy aircraft would see no light at all from above. Any chink in the curtains would receive a severe rebuke from the air raid warden on duty in the street;

"Put that light out!"

If you were in the street some distance from home when the sirens sounded you were told to make for the nearest tube station and stay down there until the all clear was given. Makeshift beds were made up along the entire length of the platforms for those who needed to sleep there overnight. It was interesting to see the odd admixture of people lying alongside each other. The class system was still ever prevalent at that time but, in the makeshift set up, people who normally would never have come into contact socially found themselves bundled together to be protected by the bombing. This was one of the many ways in which the war acted as a great leveller. The strict rationing was another case: money was irrelevant, however much of it you had, you could still only have your allocated ration. In the underground station the South Kensington toff and the East End cockney came together in a sort of amiable camaraderie with two quite different accents puncturing the air. The people were certainly divided by a common language! One of the popular songs relating to the Siegfried Line: an apparently impregnable fortress constructed by the Germans along the Franco/German border was sung along the station platform. It was;

"We're going to hang out our washing on the Siegfried Line – if the Siegfried Line's still there!"

It struck me as wonderful how Londoners could always treat the worst and most dangerous period in history with a sort of waggish humour.

Another potent aspect of this period in our nation's history was the way in which propaganda – albeit for the right reasons – was used to raise the spirits of the public in 'our darkest hour'. Whenever the R.A.F. went into action against enemy aircraft or the ground force opened up against them, it was amazing how many of the enemy planes were shot down compared to how few of ours. As the saying goes 'Truth is the first casualty of war!' Newsreels, films, radio and the press were routinely censored to exclude any material that might depress the spirits of the people. Public entertainment in the cinemas and radio – this was before the arrival of television on any scale – constantly depicted events in an optimistic light to reinforce Churchill's message that the British people were made of an impregnable material that could not be broken. Just how true this would be if we had actually been occupied, as the rest of Europe was, we will never know. The message served its purpose well at the time. The 1944 film of Shakespeare's 'Henry V' featuring Lawrence Olivier was a prime example of the sort of galvanising rubric we became used. To. Stirring speeches were aimed at the enemy propaganda, which sought to depict Britain as a spent force.

"His jest will savour but of shallow wit, when thousands weep more than did laugh at it"

And, Richard II;

"This royal throne of kings, this sceptered isle, this fortress built by nature for herself, against infection and the hand of war, this happy breed of men, this little world, this precious stone set in the silver sea, this blessed plot, this earth, this realm - this England"

(John of Gaunt)

This was some of the stirring fare served up to us on the radio, in newspapers and books and at the cinema. Looking back on some of the Pathe newsreels now, much of it seems overblown but, at the time, it was what we needed to keep us and our hopes alive – Dr Goebbels was not the only one skilled in the art of propaganda.

Wistful reflection –
The 'tube' was our night's B&B during the Blitz

46

Alan Rick

14 - BOMBED OUT HOUSES

One of the sights we became used to in the post 1945 period was of houses that, though still standing, were empty because of the damage caused to them by being bombed.

It was a depressing picture for the owners who had been obliged to abandon them: the foundations were deemed to be unstable due to bomb blasts and they were effectively designated uninhabitable.

For us children, however, it presented a golden opportunity for illicit adventure. We could wander through the rooms armed with 'guns' – usually a piece of wood sharpened at the end to resemble a bayonet, and act out the house to house searches we had seen on the Pathe newsreels in the cinema. Prisoners could be captured and locked in a cellar; the bathroom could act as an emergency hospital for the 'wounded' and sentries could be posted on the balcony to keep a look out for the 'enemy'.

The enemy also included the police whose job it was to ensure that no one entered these houses because they were unsafe. The house would form a deliciously secret haven. Forbidden activities could take place here free from the parental gaze.

One of them was "The Smoke". One of us would produce a packet of cigarettes, obtained by some dubious means, and the ritual 'light up' would follow. For us this was a special treat representing an entry into the adult world normally denied us. Casual posturing, copied from the famous film stars of that time, would follow, especially if there were girls present. But any attempt to replicate the 'Great Screen Kiss' was always vigorously rebuffed by the girl concerned; the permissive age had not yet arrived.

15 - BILLY BROWN OF LONDON TOWN

Many and varied were the attempts of the government during the war years to encourage, cajole or threaten us to adopt the correct behaviour or to refrain from any dangerous act in the cause of the safety of the public. Exhortations with pictures appeared in the daily press to observe the blackout regulations, a cartoon on the walls in the tube station depicting Hitler hiding under the armchair of two gossiping old ladies with the caption "Careless talk costs lives." It should surprise nobody to learn that the population of London did not take long to tire of this sort of thing necessary though it was. But relief was on hand in the form of a cartoon character who appeared in a giant billboard poster in nearly every main street in the capital. This was BILLY BROWN OF LONDON TOWN. Dressed in a neatly cut brown suit and sporting the mandatory black bowler hat, his mission was to wag his finger at us all and remind us of the proper conduct we should all follow. He was everywhere and there was no escape. His picture was accompanied by a caption. It seemed that members of the public had complained that some bus drivers had sailed past them at bus stops instead of stopping to allow them to get on. Billy Brown looked frowningly down at us all and addressed us with a smug and reproachful tone:

"Face the driver, raise your hand, you'll find that he will understand."

The temptation was too much for some wag who, during the night, added his own dry contribution:

"Of course he will you silly cuss but will he stop the bloody bus."

I imagine that Londoners roared their approval at this – one in the eye for officialdom.

---

16 - SHRAPNEL

Here is a word that has surely disappeared from the English language altogether. But in war torn London it was grimly familiar. It was the jagged scorched fragments of shells that continued to fall from the sky for some time after the end of an air raid. They were lethal and one piece would cut through you like a knife through butter if it fell upon you. We were urged to collect it from the ground and take it to a local collection centre where it would be recycled to make into more shells to be fired at enemy bombers whenever they staged another raid. We boys would retain a particularly interesting piece for our own prize collection so that we could compare the specimen at school in the playground. Needless to say we children were strictly forbidden to go out until all the shrapnel falling from the sky had had the time to fully settle and there was no more danger.

17 - SEARCHLIGHTS

An enemy bomber raid at night brought our ground based heavy guns into action in an attempt to shoot them down. As the aircraft could not be seen in the darkened sky, they first had to be spotted by giant searchlights operated from the ground. These were operated in pairs. This shot two parallel beams into the sky like two long fingers and the aim was to pin the aircraft in the space where the two fingers crossed. It could then be shot down easily because to escape from this trap was quite difficult for the pilot.

The reactions to all this differed greatly between the adults and us children. We, of course, thought the whole thing was great fun; we begged not to sleep in the Anderson shelter dug into our garden; we were keen to watch the search lights from our bedroom window oblivious to the danger to the German pilot who had the bad luck to be caught in them and then shot down. We were brought down to earth by grandma who urged us to think of the pilot's family and children when he did not return home. I think this point did sink in at the time, if only temporarily but it shows how the same experience is seen differently through the eyes of adults and through those of children. Richmal Crompton in her Just William knew this.

18 – TRAINS – A LOST ROMANCE

Seated on the platform of Manchester Piccadilly station the other day, watching the trains arrive and depart, my eyes misted over as I remembered the trains of my boyhood. The trains I recall were steam driven "puffers" and had a certain romance for us boys that the modern diesel engines could never have. The stock answer to the question "what do you want to be when you grow up?" was always "an engine driver". It is hard to imagine any boys saying that now. The thrilling, hissing sound the engine made as it cranked up; the billowing smoke from the chimney which filled the air around it and caused the train to momentarily fade from view until this white shroud cleared; the tough looking driver and his mate then shovelled coal into the furnace to maintain the power; all these were sights that held us boys in captive wonder. What a revelation was a train rushing through the countryside trailing clouds of glory behind it for about half a mile and, if we were lucky, the driver might ring the bell that warned the next station of his arrival.

The carriages had one single side corridor that ran the whole length of the train so that you could walk from one end to the other and peer into any other compartment along the way. Many a time a blushing courting couple were surprised in this way causing our immature sense to work overtime.

Encouraged by the black and white films of the time, many of which seemed to take place in a train, we boys would imagine standing in the corridor of the night train, hat slouched to one side, cigarette in mouth Humphrey Bogart style as a mysterious eastern European woman with an unpronounceable name would pass a package to us, describing herself as "agent X, we have you under observation – do not fail". We never understood what the words meant but we were hugely impressed.

Often, we would stand on the bridge that crossed the line at Tottenham Hale station and wait for the next train to come through. Then, tense with anticipation, we would stand still and allow ourselves to be completely enveloped in steam. For about five minutes we could not see each other one yard apart until the white mist cleared. I suppose the health zealots would not allow this today, but we loved it. We also collected the number of the trains for our collections.

But, a fond farewell to old "Puffing Billy", cherished companion of our childhood, the trigger for our young joy – you are sorely missed.

Now we have the diesel engine, more modern, not so noisy, easier to maintain and boring.

19 – TOTTENHAM GRAMMAR SCHOOL

Were the school days the "best days of my life" as the old saying proclaims? The question has something of the "Janus" quality; it presents two faces, one benign and the other malignant. My school was all boys and was established in the fifteenth century and then re-endowed by the Duchess of Somerset in the reign of Charles II.

The masters were, for the main part, of such a venerable age that they could have benefitted from a dose of re-endowment themselves. There were some glorious eccentrics among them, who constantly entertained with their odd mannerisms and quirky statements. There was the Latin master who, when asked why we could not drop Latin, peered through his spectacles at the offending boy as if examining some exotic species in a laboratory and replied "you do not drop Latin, Hamilton, Latin drops you"

I used to hope that mathematics would drop me, but it insisted on clinging to me like some malevolent harpy. But I was compensated when, in my final year, I lifted the annual Language Prize for French and German. I must mention the intrepid Hamilton again or his heroic though ultimately doomed attempt to introduce democracy into our school. He addressed a group of us in the Quad with the following stirring clarion call to action;

"What this school needs is Democracy!"

This sounded like dangerous stuff to us, but we were intrigued.

"What's that then?" enquired a boy from the front row.

"Well it's when two sides sit down at a table opposite each other and have negotiations"

"What's that then?"

"Well it's a sort of argument but without a punch-up". Hamilton now got into his stride. "Both sides then say what they reckon should happen and in the end they have an agreement"

Many doubts were expressed about the likelihood of anything like an agreement in such an authoritarian institution as the one we all belonged to but, in the end, it was decided that Hamilton would lead the project as our spokesman at the beginning of the next History lesson. The History master always wore that distant other worldly look when being spoken to so that it was impossible to tell if he was even listening. He drifted into the class and reminded us that "I believe that we were discussing the causes of the French Revolution last time". As if driven by a piston, Hamilton's hand shot up.

"Yes Hamilton, what is it?" The worldly look had taken over and the master's gaze was fixed on a point somewhere over Hamilton's head.

"We have all been discussing the question of democracy in this school and think that there should be a procedure the boys and masters could use, which I reckon is ....."

"Sit down Hamilton, before you make a damn fool of yourself".

In this way were the green shoots of democracy cut down in their infancy and no more was heard of it.

"Harry" Wright, the Art master was reputed to be mad; this was not a problem for us boys: we thought that Art masters were supposed to be unhinged – something to do with creative genius, but some of his ideas on teaching went far beyond the bounds of reason. He insisted that the way to appreciate symmetry and form was to draw boxes. Thus we spent the whole of the first year drawing boxes which had a limited aesthetic appeal. It was said, and he confirmed it, that he would wake up his wife in the middle of the night to observe the moon. He would line it up in his vision with a pencil to show how symmetrical it was. It was not recorded how his wife reacted to all this, but they were no longer together when we knew him.

The Deputy Head, Dr Williman, had a voice which could shatter glass. He would stand at the end of a long corridor and bawl out "boy" whom he had spotted with his tie and inch or two out of plumb.

The Headmaster was rarely seen around the corridors but a fearsome sight when he was. Shrouded in a black gown and topped with a mortar board, he looked like a huge black beetle on the prowl for some quarry. It was best to keep out of his way. The only teaching he did was to take the first form every Friday afternoon for Religious Instruction. It was when I failed to recite the Ten Commandments after a lesson on the subject that I was caned for the first time. The second time was for truancy.

Morning Assembly resembled a medieval pageant. Two rows of black beetles seated on a raised stage like some sort of spectral conference. Not a limb stirred as the Headmaster gave his address. This was a short address in Latin, but this was an odd anomaly as the newly arrived first formers sat uncomprehending. They had not started to learn the language.

Altogether an odd period in my life with an almost crazed obsession with competitive sport, but it did manage somehow to introduce me to the Arts for which I am grateful to them all – even to Harry Wright with his boxes.

20 – WHATEVER HAPPENED TO DODSON AND FOGG?

Yes indeed, what did happen to that solicitor's office of popular imagination – the dust covered one so vividly bought to life in the novels of Charles Dickens?

A waged man about town now.

Alan Rick

Recent observation has bought me into contact with its hugely expanded successor, a bland, hygienic world of wall to wall carpeting. Word processor screens, coffee machines and an almost complete absence of paper and eccentricity – Aldous Huxley rather than Dickens is the spokesman for all this a "Brave New World" with any interesting wrinkles finely ironed out.

On leaving school I had about a month to spare before being called up for National Service in the Army. The best plan was to take a temporary job to earn some money and in this way I gained some useful insight of the places where solicitors and barristers practise – in that black robed heart of the profession – the area covering the Inns of Court and Chancery Lane in London and in particular, Bedford Row at the back of High Holborn. The office where two partners practiced whimsicality as well as law, was in one of a row of 18th century houses in a street which looked like the film set of a Jane Austen romance. The firm had been in the house since it's foundation in 1837 and the two present partners were descended in direct line from the original two partners and bore the same two surnames. The whole outfit consisted of two partners, four typists and three clerks, one of whom spent the entire day outside the office wearing out shoe leather from place to place on the firm's business. The firm was a "general" practice meaning that it handled any type of "matter" from the conveyancing of property to the attempts of relatives to have a deceased eccentrics will set aside on the grounds that he was mad at the time he made it. The correct term for this sad condition was "testamentary incapacity". In time, I got to learn the arcane vocabulary of the law – almost a language in

59

its own right.

The whole working atmosphere had the dotty charm of an Ealing Studios film where the actual work took its place alongside – and sometimes after – discussion of that day's newspaper stories or witty anecdotes of a varied, but always proper, kind.

The office amenities were distinctly pre-yuppy. Each room was heated by a roaring open fire started by an elderly cleaning lady one hour before the arrival of the staff and maintained during the day by any member of the firm who was near enough to it to man the coal scuttle when it looked like going out. The tea or coffee was made by the office boy – a species long since made extinct by the all-purpose drinks machine – whose job also entailed visits to Twinings in the Strand when the supply seemed to be running low. The senior partner, who was 74, had first entered into the office in 1910and so had his telephone. They were both still there in 1955 although the telephone was beginning to look like the sort of relic that might appear on the Antiques Roadshow. It was of the type now being designer reproduced for the smart set – with a stand up "cradle" base and a separate ear piece on a hook on the wall. The whole contraption was urged into life by vigorous turning of a handle at its side, like the handle on the front of the old fashioned car of pre-war days.

In this pre-word processor era, paper tended to mount up as the ancient typewriters churned out three copies of each letter sent and filing was a major occupation for the all-purpose office boy. The shelf in the main office was able to boast a display of every account and ledger harking back in sequence to 1837. They were never taken down for fear that they could fall apart. This love of the preservation of old things simply because they were old was also reflected in the property deeds –some of them beautifully hand written – which adorned any shelf or office space around the firm that was not being actually used. I remember blowing the dust off an old Deed of Conveyance when I took it down from its resting place on a shelf. "Good Lord" exclaimed the senior partner "nobody has moved that Deed since it was executed". The date on it was 1932, but I was not at all surprised.

Typists at that time were difficult to find and to keep. The office started, in theory, at half past nine. In practice, they would start to arrive in instalments from about five to ten onwards and then some would manage to beat the partners to it. The "lunch hour" was similarly elastic, but again provided she got back before three o'clock a typist had a fair chance of beating the boss to it again.

Anyone who peeped into the office on any day when some stirring national or international event had just erupted could be excused for wondering if he had wandered into a debating society by mistake. The clatter of cups and the smoke of briar pipes – not at all taboo then - was accompanied by clash of opinions and sturdy argument. During the Suez Crisis of 1956, the office resembled the House of Commons in miniature from the senior partner downwards. Somehow the work was done, the client's interests were well served, but work was not all. There was always time to live, to joke and to stop and stare.

How does the modern legal factory compare with all this? It is probably more slickly efficient – it should be with all its technology – it is probably cleaner and certainly brisker and more focussed as the staff hurry earnestly through its uniform and sanitised corridors but where is the humanity and the charm and the humour?

In all this single minded pursuit of the end product it seems to have lost something that dotty old office possessed. A lightness of touch, an interest in the unusual and a refusal to take itself too seriously.

21 – THE UNMARTIAL SPIRIT

My own angst ridden adolescence had its share of farce and my two years of unmartial National Service in the Army were no exception – a lengthy exercise in human futility in an attempt to turn me into a soldier. On being posted to Egypt I remember thinking how unwise the government was to entrust the Suez Canal into my hands.

It was a dark cold day in January when I reported to Aldershot for the initial fourteen weeks training. It seemed to me like the unfolding of a nightmare, the tramp of boots, the barking of orders, the general air of profanity and the sight of grown men snapping to attention with a funny little salute. This was a culture shock to a young man who had never heard a swear word uttered in his own family circle.

We all reported to be "kitted out" which meant that, within the space of an hour, each one of us was weighed down with blankets, boots, webbing, mess tins, uniform and a .303 rifle. I could not believe this was actually happening to me and would have jumped into a hole had I been able to find one big enough.

We had to undergo a process called "documentation". This consisted of filling up a form – a kind of resume of my entire life to date and which would end up on the regimental sergeant major's desk. I was intrigued by the section requiring me to state my occupation prior to call up. This was a problem as I had not had one – I was expecting to read for a university degree when the army rudely interrupted the process. I beckoned to the duty corporal and told him I could not fill in this section as it did not apply. He was aghast. He eyed me as if I was a dangerous subversive element. "You must enter an occupation" he barked. "But I can't do that because I've never had one" I countered plaintively. His face registered panic and hostility in equal measure. "This is Army form 496" he roared "You can't leave blanks – it has to be filled up". "But what with? I've never had a job". "Well just put anything down" he sighed. Suddenly inspiration struck. Slowly and deliberately against the word "occupation" I entered "gentleman". Later that day I was to learn the first golden rule – never try to be funny in the Army – you cannot win.

Martial bearing,-Unmartial Spirit

Alan Rick

In due course the door of the billet burst open and in came the RSM – six feet tall, constructed like a stone building and with a voice that could blow a hole in a wall. He had my form in his hands and did not seem a happy man. He required to know – in a tone that made it clear that his enquiry was not a multiple choice question "which one of you is S/22624917 Rick"? "It is I" I gamely volunteered. He fixed me with a stare. He was clearly not impressed with what he saw and intoned in a voice of mock irony "we appear to 'ave a member of the more exalted echelons in our midst". My explanation fell on deaf ears. "I do 'ope you will forgive me" he continued, his eyes gleaming with menace "but you see I 'appen to suffer from an unfortunate ailment – I've no sense of humour" he roared straight into my ear.

Later that night in the cookhouse and about five hundred peeled potatoes later, he visited me on his rounds. Apologising for not being able to provide me with an occupation "more commensurate with your station in life" I was ordered to get the whole sack of potatoes peeled by breakfast. Just an incident in my youth, but what a voyage of discovery!

23 – A NIGHT IN A SAND DUNE

For some unaccountable reason my fourteen weeks initial training at Aldershot was held to have made me fit for active service abroad in one of Britain's 1950s hotspots. The arena in question was Egypt where the Fedayeen, the Egyptian underground movement dedicated to the expelling of the British occupation force from their country, was operating in a way that made me feel very uncomfortable.

The year was 1953 and, the King having died the previous year, Princess Elizabeth had just been crowned the new monarch and parties to celebrate the event were being staged in all parts of the Suez Canal zone. Needless to say, manna from heaven, in the shape of barrels of beer, was being poured down thirsty soldiers' throats and cries of "God bless you ma'am" rent the desert air at frequent intervals.

My own contribution to the general bacchanalia was to imbibe rather more of the lubricant than was wise in a tropical climate. The time to make my way, with two similarly inebriated friends back to our own camp arrived. We set out, arms around each other's shoulders, to walk across the seemingly unending expanse of the desert in a state of blissful haze. I should mention that, in the event of a sandstorm, sand dunes of up to 6-8 feet in depth are created. Down one of these I suddenly fell and found myself lying on my back looking up at the stars on a cloudless Middle-Eastern night. My companions, not having any idea where I had gone, had continued on their way without me.

I must have been asleep for some time because when I came too I became conscious of the stern faces of two of the military police peering down at me. This was not a good omen – the red caps were not noted for their amiable spirit and questions would follow. Rescued from the depths of the dune, I was required to explain my presence in it. This was not possible, as I could remember nothing from the night before. I was asked to produce my paybook. This was the book that had the details of a soldier's identity and it was an offence not to have it on you. I had already committed that offence because my paybook was lost somewhere in the sands of the desert. Establishing my identity was also a problem as the night's revels had addled my powers of recall.

In answer to the question, "Who are you?" I replied "Napoleon".

Military Police are not noted for their sense of humour and I was thrust firmly into their vehicle and driven back to my camp where I promptly fell asleep.

Came the dawn and I was informed that I had been charged with an impressive array of offences and was to parade before the commanding officer at 10.00am. At the appointed time, I was marched into his office by one of the redcaps – a corporal of particularly repellent demeanour – to find the C.O. seated impassively at his desk. He wore a look of world-weary resignation - he was used to erring miscreants appearing before him.

"What is the charge, Corporal?" he enquired in a languid tone.

The Corporal read out the charge. "Conduct unbecoming and prejudicial to good order and military discipline in that he;

one, was found lying flat out at the bottom of a sand dune under the influence of a substance which appeared to be of an intoxicating nature;

two, was not in possession of his paybook, in contravention of Army Council instructions requiring him to carry it at all times;

and, **three**, he was not able to establish his identity and when asked replied 'Napoleon' which proved to be incorrect, Sir"

This brought a slight elevation to the CO's eyebrows, and he asked the Corporal to wait outside as he wished to deal with the case himself - without witnesses.

Finding ourselves alone, the CO eyed me curiously. It had occurred to him that my surname was rather unusual.

"Are you, by any chance, related to Colonel Rick?"

"Yes Sir – he is my father" I replied.

"We served together in Benghazi." the CO continued "I don't imagine he would be very impressed with this little caper of yours – do you?"

"No Sir," I replied.

"What on earth made you do it?"

This was my chance to play the patriotic card – surely the Queen's Coronation would supply justification for a little exuberance.

"Well Sir – we were all drinking the health of the new monarch and wishing her a long reign."

"That is commendable of course," said the CO with a wry smile, "but I hardly think that laid flat out at the bottom of a sand dune would be quite what Her Majesty had in mind".

I murmured my assent and awaited the outcome.

Looking at the charge sheet, he pointed out that an entry would have to be made in the space that said *punishment awarded*.

He wrote in the space *reprimanded* – looked up at me and said "Matter dealt with I think. Off you go."

Nepotism was alive and well.

Cpl Boyden, me and knees of the desert.

24 – THE MODEL HARRIDAN

Some years ago, I sat beside Derwentwater near Keswick, contentedly smoking a pipe. A peaceful scene that was suddenly shattered by the approach of a fierce-looking woman who bore down upon me exclaiming loudly and menacingly waving her walking stick. Fearing that the gates of Hell had been opened and I was about to be admitted. I enquired with feigned humility;

"What have I done wrong?"

I must now interrupt this narration with a serious health warning, there is throughout the land a deadly virus called A.S.V. - full glossary term is *Anti-Smoking Virus*. The symptoms shown by a sufferer in the advanced stages of the disease are quite alarming and have been known to lead to violence. They include a near apoplectic reddening of the countenance, staring eyes and a tendency to jab a finger into the chest of another as they make a moral point concerning the health of the environment. Indeed, there is nothing more alarming than an A.S.V sufferer in the midst of a fit of morality. Up until now, there is no known cure apart from complete ostracism.

The particular lady who bore down on me was of the environmentalist persuasion.

"Have you any idea what you are doing to the environment with your pipe – launching smoke into the air?" she thundered. I looked up at a beautiful clear sky and the entirely smoke-free air for miles around.

"The environment seems to be taking care of itself well enough" I mildly countered. "I don't see any birds dropping out of the sky. To my surprise, and relief, she veered off in another direction leaving me to smoke my pipe in peace.

During the course of my soporific reflection, I remembered an incident I had been involved in some time before. I was cycling gently through Middleton when, caught at the lights on red, I found myself behind a car. There was, of course, no chance for me to reposition myself as there were vehicles behind me and on both sides. I was in a trap.

Suddenly, the car in front, still stationary, belched out from its exhaust pipe a thick, dense cloud of blue smoke straight into my face and I suppose into my lungs. Looking back on this event is occurs to me that this cloud burst must have been the equivalent of about a hundred well filled pipes or a thousand cigarettes. As if to compound the irony, the driver had a notice in his back window which required the public at large to *"Have a care for the air we breathe – give up smoking"*.

Since we are constantly being warned from all sides of the health lobby of the danger to our health of smoking, - rightly enough I suppose. I look forward, with interest to legislation being passed through Parliament to shut down the entire car industry in the interests of our health. I think we will wait in vain for that – the vested business and economic interests are far too powerful.

25 – TUBBY MULLINS

Tubby Mullins was not the life and soul of any party! He was not a National Serviceman like the rest of us, but a left-over from the Second World War with one stripe – and an impressive array of tattoos on his arm to show for it. In the NAAFI canteen in the evening, when we regaled each other as best we could in a desert camp with nothing else to do, Tubby would sit there, sphinx-like, and not say a word all evening. The only sign of life was a slow and laborious raising of his pint to his lips, and an occasional grunt to the rest of us to confirm that he was still there. To say that Tubby was glum would be to attribute more animation to him than was the case. A fish on a slab would seem excited compared to Tubby and his lumbering steps to the bar would make a tortoise look like an Olympic sprinter.

Tubby never smiled; the rest of us told a whole range of jokes and anecdotes, but these were completely lost on Tubby, who would just stare balefully into space.

One evening, we were interrupted by the Duty Officer; a fresh-faced young man with a plummy public school voice with news that an urgent supply of equipment was to be delivered to a camp a few miles across the desert. Tubby would drive, but because the Fedayeen – the Egyptian terrorist underground – was active, he had to be accompanied by an armed escort. This was to be my role.

Armed with a sten gun, I took my place beside Tubby in the open vehicle. We set off across the sandy waste of the

Sinai Desert, until there was nothing else in sight in any direction. Suddenly, the sky was obliterated by the Khamseen, a sandstorm the like of which we Europeans had never seen. The sand of the desert was lifted into the air by violent and hot winds, causing it to swirl in a solid mass as if engaged in some manic dance. There was nothing to be done but hide under the vehicle until it had passed over us and veered off into the distance, leaving the air around us clear again.

Suddenly Tubby rolled over on his side and glumly intoned "gotta laugh aintcher".

This from a man who had never been known to laugh in his life.

26 – A MOMENT TO SAVOUR

This was a moment I would remember for a long time. So I thought, as I placed my suitcase on the ground beside a rural bus stop and gazed back at the gate of the camp that had closed behind me some ten minutes before. I had, after all, waited for two years for this and now that it had arrived it was taking some time to fully sink in…

Through the gates I saw, now with some amusement, the strange antics of National Service going about its daily routine, the parade on the square, the sergeant with a voice that could shatter glass and the forlorn effort of a newly arrived soldier to strip and re-assemble a bren gun.

"They were rather foolish to place one of those things in my hands." I mused with a chuckle.

The bus now came into view on the floor of the valley before winding its lethargic way up the country lane towards me. Never before had the sight of a bus given me such a thrill – it was like an angel on wheels come to deliver me from the last two years spent in uniform. I looked down at the civilian clothes I was wearing. I had not seen them for twenty four months.

I greeted the startled bus conductor with a "Boy – am I glad to see you!"

I settled into a back window seat and watched the camp disappear into the distance.

#0072 - 260418 - C0 - 210/148/4 - PB - DID2182515